TALKING POLITICS WITH JESUS:

A PROCESS PERSPECTIVE ON THE SERMON ON THE MOUNT

BRUCE EPPERLY

Topical Line Drives, Volume 47

Energion Publications
Gonzalez, Florida
2022

ISBN: 978-1-63199-808-9
eISBN: 978-1-63199-809-6

Energion Publications
P. O. Box 841
Gonzalez, FL 32560

energion.com
pubs@energion.com

TABLE OF CONTENTS

POLITICS WITHOUT PARTISANSHIP

This book began with a question raised in a most unusual environment. My wife Kate and I had taken our eighty-five-pound Golden Doodle Tucker to our veterinarian. In the course of the checkup, the veterinarian noticed the book I brought with me, John Howard Yoder's *The Politics of Jesus* and inquired, "Was Jesus a liberal or a conservative?" Being a theologian, I couldn't resist responding, "I don't think Jesus would be a Republican or Democrat. He'd be critical of both political parties. But he would align himself with the poor and powerless, social outcasts, and persons who can't afford health care. He wouldn't oppose capitalism provided it serves the common good."

About the same time, one of our congregants asked me to focus on "the politics of Jesus" as the topic of our weekly theological reflection seminar. As I pondered Jesus' politics with a group of participants from various denominational backgrounds, I turned to the Sermon on the Mount, a collection of Jesus' most provocative ethical statements as the lens through which to understand Jesus' political perspective in his time and the relevance of Jesus' message to our twenty-first-century political context. Although Jesus did not advocate specific political policies, the Sermon on the Mount reflects his vision of community, politics, and civic conversation. A third event occurred in the course of our seminar: the Coronavirus (COVID-19 pandemic) which forced us to conduct our final classes on Zoom and suspend our worship services, but more importantly challenged virtually every assumption we had about the stability and security of the American way of life and its images of progress and control. These American assumptions were further challenged by the deaths of George Floyd, the shooting of Jacob Blake, Breonna Taylor, and others, bringing to light the systemic injustices faced by persons of color, grounded in America's "original sin" of slavery and racism.

From these two conversations as well as the realities of protest and pandemic, this book emerged as a theological and spiritual dialogue with Jesus. If Jesus is relevant to our world today, he must have something to say about the current chaos of our national and international politics as well as our response to the Coronavirus pandemic and structural racism. While not giving us all the answers, Jesus' words provide a pathway through the wilderness of incivility, injustice, and incoherence. They give us hope in a time of upheaval. Jesus' upside-down realm challenges every political and economic system to seek a "more perfect union" and invites us to follow, as Abraham Lincoln counseled, "the better angels of our nature" even when we are tempted to succumb to the idolatry of family, religion, or nation first.

The Sermon on the Mount is both timeless and timely in guiding our political and ethical decision-making. Though located in the first-century Roman occupation of Judea, Jesus' Sermon is as current as this morning's newsfeed. My approach to the Sermon on the Mount is informed by current New Testament scholarship as well as process-relational theology. Together, they help us to see the Sermon on the Mount in terms of concrete experience rather than abstract theological doctrines or legalistic rules. It is my hope that these brief meditations will inspire you to consider God's vision for political involvement and the relationship of faith and politics.

I want to express my gratitude to the participants of the theological reflection group, meeting every Wednesday at South Congregational Church, United Church of Christ, in Centerville, Massachusetts. I also want to thank my publisher Henry Neufeld for his commitment to lay and professional theology and my editor Chris Eyre, who brings insights from Great Britain to this very North American author. This text is dedicated to my grandchildren Jack and James and children all over the world with hope that our decisions might create a beautiful world in which city streets and country roads resound with joy.

CHAPTER ONE

THE REAL POLITICS OF JESUS' WORLD[1]

The parent of process theology Alfred North Whitehead asserts that the whole universe conspires to create each moment of experience. Though Whitehead also notes that religion begins in solitude, he equally affirms the dynamic and relational nature of life. Whitehead would have approved of the affirmation attributed to Nicolas of Cusa and Saint Bonaventure: God is a circle whose center is everywhere and whose circumference is nowhere. Each moment of life and every creature is God-saturated. The place where I stand is Beth-El, a unique gateway to God, as the patriarch Jacob discovers, but all places are also interconnected icons of divine activity.

Locality and universality are intimately connected. We need to think globally and act locally. We also need to recognize with USA Speaker of the House, Tip O'Neill that while all politics is local, ethical reflection drives us from self-interest to world loyalty. Jesus' political vision is profoundly local, grounded in his experience as a first-century Jew growing up under Roman military occupation Romans. Yet, from the prison house of first-century political occupation, Jesus experienced God's movements in all creation and shared a vision applicable to humankind in every social, political, and technological context.

To talk politics with Jesus, we need to begin with the fact that he was a first-century Jew, who never experienced a moment of political freedom. He was born into a proud and chosen people, a child of Abraham, Moses, and the prophets as well as Mary and Joseph. But, unlike citizens of liberal democracies, he had neither political power nor influence in the political process. He spent his whole life under the thumb of the Empire. While Rome touted the "Pax Romana," Roman peace was achieved through terror, either

---

1 Much of this chapter is inspired by Marcus Borg and N.T. Wright, *The Meaning of Jesus: Two Visions* (New York: HarperOne, 2007), John Dominic Crossan, *Jesus: A Revolutionary Biography* (New York: HarperSanFrancisco, 1994), Obery Hendricks, *The Politics of Jesus* (New York: Doubleday Books, 2006), Howard Thurman, *Jesus and the Disinherited* (Boston: Beacon Press, 1996).

directly meted out by the Roman military or local sovereigns, such as Herod, who established police states, characterized by spying, imprisonment, and torture. Jesus and his fellow citizens could be impressed into servitude by the whim of any military official. They paid taxes without representation not only to Rome but also to the religious authorities in Jerusalem, who demanded fees for services and ostracized anyone who could not pay for religious rites of blessing and purification.

Jesus' family belonged to the salt of the earth, common folk, who were easily and often crushed underfoot by the powers that be. Among the majority poor, the first century was a time of great expectation. Politically powerless, some dreamed of a military savior, a Messiah modeled after the great King David, who would descend from the heavens, destroying the Roman occupation forces. They imagined a final God-ordained military victory similar to the Maccabean Revolt (167-160 BCE), temporarily displacing the Greek regime under Antiochus IV. Others withdrew from society entirely, seeking personal and communal purity as paving the way for the restoration of Israel as a light to the nations. John the Baptist and, perhaps, Jesus himself were influenced by the Qumran community, the creators of what we know as the Dead Sea Scrolls, which sought to prepare for the coming Messiah through transformed ethical and spiritual practices.

Common people both respected and resented the religious leaders of their time. Like some of today's conservative Christian leaders, many Jewish religious authorities aligned themselves with Rome, believing that the conflation of religion and power, centered on the Jerusalem Temple, would ensure survival for the nation and wealth for the favored few. As in later Christian history, such alignments are always spiritually ambiguous. When Constantine rode into Rome with the Christian flag, he paved the way for a global religion. He also reduced Christianity to good citizenship, encouraged social prejudice, and promoted a preferential option for the wealthy and powerful. Constantine's Christian followers joined church and state to domesticate Jesus' radical message. They defined Christianity in terms of assenting to creedal formulae, obedience to religious authorities, and the aspiration to be good citizens who followed social and political norms that would have been an anathema to Jesus: military violence, crusades, slavery, ecclesiastical wealth, and political power, racism, sexism, and homophobia.

Still, beneath the compromises of the Jerusalem religious leaders was the prophetic dream of an alternative reality of "justice rolling down like waters, and righteousness like an ever-flowing stream." (Amos 5:24) In Jesus' time, people still remembered God's promise that Israel would be a light to the nations, a spiritual center for humankind. This spiritual restlessness and dream of an alternative reality are captured in Mary's radical hymn of praise:

> God's mercy is for those who fear God
> from generation to generation.
> God has shown strength with his divine arm;
> God has scattered the proud in the thoughts of their hearts.
> God has brought down the powerful from their thrones,
> and lifted up the lowly;
> God has filled the hungry with good things,
> and sent the rich away empty.
> God has helped his servant Israel,
> in remembrance of divine mercy,
> according to the promise God made to our ancestors,
> to Abraham and to his descendants forever.
> (Luke 1:50-55)

In this restless time, "the hopes and fears of all the years" were surely present in the hearts of Jesus' listeners as he shared his vision of an upside-down realm in words we have come to know as the Sermon on the Mount. Jesus' message was spiritual, advocating a new way of looking at the world, and ethical decision-making, based on embodying God's vision in daily life. Jesus' counsel was also political. A world of transformed values leads to transformed behaviors and alternative forms of citizenship that threaten the political and religious machinations grounded in violence, injustice, and identification of God and nation.

Jesus' irenic vision was dangerous to the powerful. The religious leaders plotted his death, and eventually he fell victim to the joint forces of religion and government. The way of Caesar coopted prophetic religion and personal piety in its quest to destroy

6

Jesus and his movement. Yet, as Alfred North Whitehead notes, the Galilean vision persists, embodied in the moral and spiritual arcs of history, which stand in judgment of every political system, challenging nations and their citizens "to do justice, and to love kindness, and walk humbly with your God." (Micah 6:8)

The Sermon on the Mount incarnates the prophetic dream of God's realm "on earth as it is in heaven" and challenges us to embody God's realm of Shalom in the hardscrabble world of economics, law, politics, and foreign policy. From his position of political powerlessness, Jesus is silent in terms of specific initiatives in public policy. Instead, Jesus shows us how to live faithfully as citizens whose values challenge our political leaders to seek justice, welcome strangers, promote peaceful resolution to conflict, and provide resources for vulnerable persons.

The Sermon on the Mount, born of Jesus' own restless quest to embody God's realm in every dimension of life, challenges every form of Christianity that puts power above love, economics over justice, and violence before peacemaking. The God of the Sermon is the fellow sufferer who understands and the loving companion who celebrates. Not a ruler on high, or a Caesar on earth, Jesus' Sermon presents a vision of divine power as relational, invitational, inspirational, empowering us to become God's companions in healing the world.

CHAPTER TWO

THE UPSIDE-DOWN WORLD
OF THE BEATITUDES

(Matthew 5:1-12)

"With blessings like these who needs curses!" was the response of a friend when she heard I would be lecturing on Jesus' Beatitudes. The Sermon on the Mount begins with a series of unusual and countercultural blessings that must have confused and scandalized his audience. They scandalize us today. Imagine the following states as being joyful, blessed, or happy:

- Poverty of spirit
- Grief
- Meekness
- Passion for justice
- Mercy
- Purity of heart
- Persecution

At first sight, these blessings contradict the popular connection of spirituality with peace of mind, contentment, equanimity, success, and prosperity. Further, they challenge our concept of blessedness in terms of individual fortune and well-being. There is no prosperity gospel in Jesus' blessings, nor is there an affirmation of capitalism as the Christian way of life.

Jesus' Beatitudes are a faith for the restless, searching, passionate, and adventurous spirit. Like the prophets of old, those who are blessed experience a divine restlessness, a sense of utter dependence on God and the support of others, and a willingness to experience power as relational and sacrificial rather than coercive and domineering.

Luke's Gospel speaks of the poor being blessed (Luke 6:20), while Matthew adds poor in spirit. Luke's economic poverty is often spiritualized by readers of Matthew, leading them to separate spirituality and politics and assume that faith is primarily a matter of individual spiritual growth and personal relationships. In contrast to the purely spiritual and apolitical approach to the Beatitudes, both gospels have a preferential option for the dispossessed and marginalized. Both gospels recognize what the vulnerable know first-hand. We can't go it alone. We need the kindness of strangers, a healthy environment, economic opportunity, and just treatment to survive in a contradictory social order. The poor in spirit struggle for self-esteem in a world in which their backs are against the wall. They know that whatever they achieve comes by way of God's grace empowering and energizing them and not their own solitary efforts. No applause for self-made people. No privileging of legacy children, believing that their parents' largesse entitles them to preferential treatment in terms of taxation, higher education, or legal status. We are all in this together. To the one we call Savior, the illusion of individual success is the greatest danger to personal spirituality and economic justice.

Those who mourn know their lives to be fragile and incomplete. A friend noted that "I expected to be the first one to die. When my wife died, I lost something precious, a part of me died, too!" Grief is grounded in the collapse of rituals and relationships, of those realities that nurture the spirit and give meaning to our lives. Jesus mourns the death of Lazarus and the godlessness of his nation's capital. The prophets lament dishonesty and fraud among the nation's political and religious leaders. They experience the divine pathos, God's suffering with the vulnerable, marginalized, and dispossessed. Flowing with their own tears are the tears of divine empathy. The prophets empathize with Langston Hughes' mournful recognition that the impact of slavery still shapes the lives of African Americans, "America never was America for me." We mourn the hundreds of thousands of lives lost, including a disproportional percentage of persons of color, during the pandemic as well as our nation's continuing systemic injustice and racism.

Another friend, now two years after his wife's death, states: "I'm glad now I'm the one who survived. I took on the grief she would have felt. I wouldn't have grieved without our love. My grief has become gratitude for the love we had and the love I still have for her."

9

God doesn't sit on the sidelines. God is the fellow sufferer who experiences the pain of the farmer grieving farm foreclosure; the widow unable to feed her children; the family bankrupted by medical expenses; the parent who must give her teenage son the "talk" about how to survive as a black male when stopped by the police; the transgendered woman bullied and berated; the four-year-old separated from her asylum-seeking parents, crying herself to sleep in a concentration camp on the USA borderlands; the First American shaman crying for a vision to save his people, the victims of genocide in the creation of a great nation; the factory worker plunged into poverty and hearing the boss say, "it's nothing personal, it's just business." Lament and grief are personal, but the personal is also the political, often the painful result of the machinations of governmental and religious leaders. God celebrates and the heavens declare God's glory, but God grieves the pain we inflict on each other and the immorality of leaders and nations. Like God, we grieve what our nation could be when we compare God's vision of Shalom, embodied in liberty and justice for all, with our current injustice, incivility, and environmental destruction. Surely God is grieving along with families who could not, as a result of the Coronavirus, sit at the bedside of dying patients as well as the indifference of political leaders who place economic interests ahead of the wellbeing of minimum wage workers. God is grieving with all victims of police brutality and injustice in the courts. The God of the Beatitudes grieves and protests the machinations of those in high places who foment civil unrest, distort medical science, and deny climate change.

The meek humbly recognize their common humanity. Different as we appear, we are one. No one better, no one entitled, no one immune from the human condition. No one separated spiritually or ethically. Jesus tells the story of God's honoring the spirituality of a sinner crying out "Lord have mercy," more than the self-righteous religiosity of the person who looks down on him. Jesus concludes the parable with the judgment, "Those who exalt themselves will be humbled; those who humble themselves will be exalted." (Luke 18: 9-14) We are all "standin' in the need of prayer" once we get beyond the illusions of power and prestige, health and ability, race and age, and morality and immorality. Ironically one of the signs of sainthood is the recognition of fallibility, imperfection, and our dependence on God for all good gifts, including our moral stature.

Those who hunger and thirst for righteousness experience the divine restlessness that judges every system as fallible, imperfect, and in need of healing. Our restless spirits reflect God's own passionate impatience with the ponderous movement of the moral and spiritual arc of history. The God of the Beatitudes is emotionally embedded in history. God's empathy births forth a divine passion for justice and intimate care for all God's children. The God of the Sermon on the Mount doesn't deal with abstractions, whether ethical or economic. God deals with the concrete realities of joy and pain and the challenges of discerning God's vision in a complicated world.

The God of the Beatitudes inspires the emergence of Bodhisattvas, Christs and Buddhas to be, who abandon the placid spirituality of heaven and nirvana until all "justice rolls down like waters and righteousness like an ever-flowing stream" (Amos 5:24) and till all creation experiences God's healing touch and every nation embraces truth and love.

Blessed are the merciful and pure-hearted, those who see beyond appearances, who challenge injustice, who have only one goal amid their many responsibilities, to do something beautiful for God. The merciful and pure-hearted fervently ask with the characters of Charles Sheldon's Social Gospel classic, *In His Steps*, "What would Jesus do?" in the classroom, polling place, picket line, and stock market. Recognizing the connection between poverty, low self-esteem, broken relationships, not to mention race and injustice in the courtrooms, they extend mercy to the incarcerated whether in our nation's prisons or borderland concentration camps. Like Bryan Stevenson, author of *Just Mercy*, they discover that death row is the crucible for faithful living. Even the convicted murderer deserves justice. When the legal system itself is unjust and in the USA, one out of every nine prisoners on death row is innocent, we experience God's protest inspiring our own.

Protest can lead to persecution. The countercultural lifestyle of the Beatitudes puts us at odds with our society's norms, religious practices, and public policies when they stand in the way of God's vision of Shalom. A prophet is seldom appreciated by the powers that be. The alternative prophetic vision threatens the unjust status quo of consumption, inequality, poverty, and war-making. Jesus' vision of open community and unbounded healing led to the cross, a profoundly political act enacted by the Roman occupying forces and their religious co-conspirators.

When I was in college, I spied a poster, highlighting a psychedelic Jesus who queried "If you were arrested for being a Christian, would there be enough evidence to convict you?" While I now chuckle at my antics among the 1960's hippies and Jesus freaks, I also must confess how far baby boomers have strayed from the idealism of phrases like "the summer of love," "make love not war," and "harmony and understanding, sympathy and trust abounding" in the dawning of the Age of Aquarius." Our reckless consumption has been a major factor in environmental destruction and climate change. We have conformed to the world of comfort and materialism. Even spirituality has become a product to be sold at workshops and televangelist revivals, urging us to "create our own realities" or "name and claim" God's prosperity with the appropriate spiritual practice and financial contribution.

Our idealism has given way to pragmatism and prosperity as "we have paved paradise and put up a parking lot." Even those of us who seek to simplify our lives and strand with the powerless must confess that we are complicit in the evils we deplore. Yet, the gift of recognizing our complicity is an antidote to judgmentalism, polarization, and incivility. As "guilty bystanders," in the words of Thomas Merton, we recognize that our privilege is bought at the price of others' poverty and powerlessness. Connected with all life in its tragic beauty and brokenness, we experience the blessings of lamentation, humility, and spiritual poverty which can become the catalyst for compassionate and caring political decision-making.

In the upside-down world of the Beatitudes, the poor are blessed and the wealthy go away empty-handed. The lost are found, seekers find their way, and our own restlessness aligns with the Restless Adventurers of God our companion and friend.

CHAPTER THREE

REVEALING LIGHT
(Matthew 5:13-16)

I can't help thinking of the children's song "This Little Light of Mine," whenever I read the words, "You are the light of the world. Let your light shine." As a child, it was one of my favorite Sunday School songs, the words inspiring optimism, empowerment, and the belief that, like the boy with the five loaves and two fish, I could make a difference.

> This little light of mine, I'm gonna let it shine...
> Won't hide it under a bushel basket (No!),
> I'm gonna let it shine...
> Everywhere I go, I'm gonna let it shine, let it shine, let
> it shine, let it shine.

Imagine the upside-down spirit of "You are the light of the world." These are the same words John's Gospel uses to describe God's world-creative light and Jesus' own identity as the "the light of the world." Imagine the response of Jesus' followers, powerless and beaten down by Roman occupation and their marginalized social status when they heard Jesus say "You are the light of the world" and then began to look at themselves and say "I am the light of the world." The Romans can do what they want with my body, but they can't dominate my spirit because God's light will eventually overcome the darkness of Rome and every other pretender to divinity.

Howard Thurman describes the power of words to transform the lives of vilified and oppressed persons. As President John Hope of Morehouse College described the young men gathered for chapel as "gentlemen," he saw himself in a new light.

> He always addressed us as "young gentlemen." What this
> term of respect meant to our faltering egos can only be under-
> stood against the backdrop of the South of the 1920's. We were
> black men in Atlanta during a period in which Georgia was
> infamous for its racial brutality. Lynchings, burning, unspeak-

13

able cruelties were the fundamentals of existence for black people. Our physical lives were of little value. Any encounter with a white person was inherently dangerous and frequently fatal. Those of us who managed to remain physically whole found our lives defined in less than human terms.[2]

In a time in which black men of all ages were addressed as "boy" and women as "Mary," President Hope reminded Thurman and his fellow students that God's image shined through their lives despite the indignities of racism. The light of God could not be extinguished by the diabolical spirit of separate but equal and Jim Crow laws. Decades later, Jesse Jackson activated that same spirit of hopeful self-affirmation when he led crowds in chanting "I am somebody." Imagine a ghetto child on the verge of interiorizing the racism of our nation, believing herself to be inferior to the proud and privileged world of whiteness, discovering that she matters, is valuable, and can do something great in her life. Today, Jesus would chant with James Brown, "Say it loud, I'm black and I'm proud" with words that remind us that "black lives matter" in their concreteness not just "all lives matter" in their abstraction.

Each Sunday in church, I share the following affirmation with our children and youth – knowing the rest of the congregation is listening – "God loves you. We love you. You matter. You can do something beautiful with your life." When you recognize that God's light shines in you, you can't demean yourself or a fellow human being, even including those whose goal is to keep you in your place.

God's light enlightens everyone. Shining through us, God's light reveals the beauty and ugliness of the world. Even the smallest glimmer of light can challenge and reveal the darkness of political and social injustice. Hidden schemes and scams are brought to light. The Empire's pretensions and prevarications are made public, their moral and spiritual bankruptcy is disclosed and disempowered.

Mated with light is salt. "You are the salt of the earth" not only describes common people, the easily stepped on and discarded. It also describes the spiritual humility that gives birth to power. Salt

---

2 Howard Thurman, *With Head and Heart: The Autobiography of Howard Thurman* (New York: Harcourt, Brace and Company, 1979), 36.

preserves and enhances. It brings forth the flavors of tradition and then transforms them into their intended purpose, actively enhancing whatever it touches.

Salt and light are political as well as individual. As the leaders of the early feminist movement asserted, the personal is the political. To see yourself in a new light – as God's salt and light – as one who is holy and active in bringing truth to the halls of power and religion challenges the vulnerable and the apathetic to move from passivity to agency, in confronting the evils of our world.

CHAPTER FOUR

POLITICS FROM THE INSIDE OUT

(Matthew 5:17-42)

When I was nine years old, I came to the altar and accepted Christ as my Savior at a small-town revival meeting. As I stood at the altar with tears in my eyes, one of the deacons queried, "Do you accept Jesus as your personal savior?" I responded with a strong "yes," and was assured that if I died later that day, I would be with Jesus in heaven. Now almost sixty years later, I realize that having a relationship with Jesus is more complicated than I was told. It's not just about heaven and how to get there, it's about bringing the values of heaven to our everyday lives and political decision-making. Accepting Jesus as your savior is not just a creedal affirmation aimed at individual salvation, but a way of life that can lead to conflict, challenge, and confrontation with the powers and principalities.

Alfred North Whitehead asserted that religion is what a person does with their solitariness. The philosopher meant that in solitude and silence we transcend the values of popular religion and culture. While we may still participate in institutional religion, we see life from a wider perspective, moving from parochial rituals and creeds to spiritual ecumenism and world loyalty. In solitude, we discover that the personal is political and that each person emerges from and contributes to their community, nation, and the world.

An Impossible Ethical Standard? The aphorisms of Matthew 5:17-48 present, at first glance, an impossible ethical standard. Speaking as the fulfillment of the eighth century BCE prophetic tradition and the Hebraic law, Jesus presents a vision in which the inner and outer lives are intimately connected. Spiritual maturity involves right behavior, reflected in following social norms related to marriage, sexual activity, almsgiving, and civility. A deeper spirituality focuses on the solitude of personal experience, often known only to God and us. In an interdependent universe, mind and body penetrate one another, our cells influence our souls and our thoughts impact our physical wellbeing. Our attitude toward social mores and behaviors can uplift or destroy. Our character is reflected in our behavior and our character is also shaped by the social and religious values of our communities.

The aphorisms of Matthew 5 are grounded in the unity of contemplation and action. The quest for the just society begins with inner transformation. We need spiritual depth to respond to the injustice of oppression with courage and patience, and to restrain the impulse to violence. When revolutionary movements focus solely on external change without concern for the inner life, they often succumb to the same authoritarianism they abhor in the oppressor. When we fail to prayerfully cultivate a sense of the holiness of the oppressor and ourselves, we add to the violence of the world. Conversely, without justice in the courthouse, marketplace, and Halls of Parliament and Congress, inner transformation is put at risk. Protest joined with prayer creates an environment of change while preserving the possibility of reconciliation.

Jesus says, "don't resist an evildoer." His ethic of peaceful non-resistance is not capitulation, but courageous self-differentiation. Jesus' pacifism is both spiritual and political. While the principle of "an eye for an eye, a tooth for a tooth," was intended to restrain violent reprisals against wrongdoers, the violence of *lex talionis* can easily escalate into all-out war. As a spiritual principle, peaceful non-resistance enables both oppressors and oppressed to find common ground. Violence, even to redress social injustice, creates chasms in our communities that cannot easily be repaired. Non-violence opens the door for prophetic healing. Political challenges are joined with recognizing the holy in those whom we oppose. Both parties are invited to affirm the "better angels" of their nature. As a political strategy, peaceful non-resistance does not preclude civil disobedience, grounded in the justness of one's cause. Rosa Parks' refusal to change seats on the bus along with sit-ins at lunch counters, protesting separate but equal water fountains, blocking entrances to nuclear power plants, and being arrested at climate change and immigration protests are acts of conscience intended to challenge the conscience of those who perpetrate violence and injustice. In the spirit of Jesus' admonition to his followers, such actions are grounded in spiritual practices that reduce the temptation to respond violently to the violence of the powers that be. Even when the damage of property occurs, such as Jesus driving out the money changers or Roman Catholic priest Daniel Berrigan burning draft files at Catonsville, Maryland, protestors scrupulously avoid harming others. Protests are a call to spiritual and political transformation. In the case of the Catonsville Nine:

> In May of 1968, Berrigan and eight other activists seized several hundred military draft records from the Selective Service office in Catonsville and then burned what they had looted in a fire fueled by homemade napalm. As the files went up in flames, the Catonsville Nine, as they became known, made impassioned statements against the war in Vietnam and then recited the Lord's Prayer.[3]

Non-violent civil disobedience has a cost. Martin Luther King goes to jail, Dan and Phil Berrigan are sentenced to prison, and Jesus is crucified by the military and religious authorities.

Jesus challenges the spiritual values of institutional religion, which practices spiritual and financial extortion from the poorest members of society, forced to buy birds and lambs for ritual sacrifices. The collusion of temple and state dishonors God and oppresses the vulnerable, already the victims of extortion by Roman tax collectors.

Freedom and relationship are at the heart of Jesus' impossible ethic. Freedom is manifest in the "going the second mile," "giving up your cloak," and "turning the other cheek." The occupying force can control my body but not my spirit. During Jesus' time, Roman soldiers could arbitrarily demand that a peasant carry their equipment up to one mile. In traveling a second mile, the peasant becomes an agent, not a victim, making a choice that implicitly challenges oppressive domination and humiliation. Giving up your cloak, when your coat is demanded by the oppressor, reflects the power of choice. Since the cloak was typically the undergarment, the subject of persecution renders himself naked, embarrassing the oppressor, making his intent to humiliate laughable. Turning the other cheek ironically transforms the victim into an agent of destiny, forcing the perpetrator to make an ethical decision. How

---

3 https://progressive.org/dispatches/dan-berrigan-priest-burned-draft-cards-taunted-fbi/

far will the oppressor go to take control of the situation? Will the oppressor stoop to gratuitous violence, thus becoming the moral inferior of the ones they look down upon?

The behaviors of others do not have to determine our inner lives. In the midst of the diabolical machinations of the Third Reich, Viktor Frankl asserted that "everything can be taken from a man but one thing: the last of the human freedoms—to choose one's attitude in any given set of circumstances, to choose one's own way." Frankl continues, "when we can no longer change the situation, we can change ourselves."

Protest was not an option for Jesus' fellow citizens. Nor could inmates in Nazi concentration camps go on strike. Their survival depended on inner strength. In democracies, as fragile they seem at times, we can be more confrontational than persons living in dictatorships in responding to the injustices perpetrated by politicians and business leaders. With African American activist Angela Davis, we can assert, "I'm no longer accepting the things I cannot change. I am challenging the things I cannot accept."

The words of Matthew 5 challenge us to follow Jesus' path of growing in wisdom and stature. As we will see in the next chapter, the inner journey ends with a different kind of perfection, not the perfection of purity or separation from moral and spiritual inferiors, but the fallible human quest to imitate the all-inclusive love of the One who guides our path.

CHAPTER FIVE

ALL-EMBRACING LOVE

(Matthew 5:43-48)

And Jesus spoke on the mountain, "Be perfect, therefore, as your Father in heaven is perfect." (Matthew 5:48) Jesus' admonition to his very imperfect followers haunts everyone who seeks to join the way of Jesus. What does it mean to be perfect? Is the command to be perfect just another impossible demand for obviously imperfect and fallible persons like us and our institutions? Or, is it aspirational, challenging us to go beyond self-interest to sacrificial living and planetary care and from exclusion to inclusion? Inspired by a similar restlessness of spirit, the Preamble to the Constitution of the United States of America states:

> We the People of the United States, in Order to form a more perfect Union, establish Justice, insure domestic Tranquility, provide for the common defence, promote the general Welfare, and secure the Blessings of Liberty to ourselves and our Posterity, do ordain and establish this Constitution for the United States of America.

There is no clear consensus what the framers of the USA Constitution meant. Did they mean the movement from individual states toward a unified government? Or did they imagine a polestar that would constantly provoke a spiritual and political restlessness? A vision of what the USA, God's "almost chosen people," as Abraham Lincoln noted, could become? Did the founding parents recognize that their best efforts in creating a new nation fell short of their ultimate aspiration for a nation affirming "liberty and justice for all" and would constantly challenge their successors to expand this vision to include all people and not just white males?

Jesus' challenge for us to seek perfection is real in our personal and political lives. The horizon charted by the Galilean healer takes us beyond the purity and legalism that set apart sinners from the righteous ones in Jesus' time. In fact, perfection, defined as wholeness and inclusive hospitality, takes us in the opposite direction, plunging us into the messy maelstrom of history, compromise, conflict, and idealism. Perfection is incarnational, sacrificing as Jesus did our "otherness" to live in solidarity with all creation, including wayward persons and their political institutions.

Our quest for perfection is grounded in our affirmation of divine providence and the recognition, in the words of Unitarian pastor Theodore Parker that history is driven by an immanent moral arc, a far horizon embedded in our political processes that lures us toward God's vision of what we can be as nations and individuals. For Jesus, our quest for perfection motivates us to be global persons, growing in wisdom and stature, seeking to embody Godlike virtues, becoming like the God we worship. On the mountain, Jesus visualizes God in terms of inclusion:

> You have heard that it was said, 'You shall love your neighbor and hate your enemy.' But I say to you, Love your enemies and pray for those who persecute you, so that you may be children of your Father in heaven; for he makes his sun rise on the evil and on the good, and sends rain on the righteous and on the unrighteous. For if you love those who love you, what reward do you have? Do not even the tax collectors do the same? And if you greet only your brothers and sisters, what more are you doing than others? Do not even the Gentiles do the same? Be perfect, therefore, as your heavenly Father is perfect.

God is a circle whose center is everywhere and whose circumference is nowhere. God has no boundaries or outside either to God's love or creativity. God compassionately embraces every creature, even those who politics and economics God must challenge, and the totality of the universe. God is present in all things, as the source of possibility and the energy of achievement. Conversely, all things are present in God, who gives life to every creature in God's ever-expanding experience of the universe. God loves all creation, without exception, and is willing to sacrifice Godself to heal the world. (John 3:16)

The Greek philosopher Xenophanes stated that "if horses had gods, they would look like horses." Jesus' aim at perfection is grounded in a similar understanding of human nature. We become conformed to our visions of God, not just the bearded old man in the heavens but the divinity present in our daily decision-making and public policies. If our God is authoritarian and legalistic in nature, we will understand human life in terms of obedience and punishment. If we see God as primarily as an absolute sovereign, then we will worship power and create institutions that rule by compulsion, separating friends and enemies in this life and beyond. In contrast, if we imagine God as creative and adventurous, loving diversity, and actively present in our world, we will promote creativity, freedom, and diversity in our relationships and the body politic. We will build bridges rather than walls and seek partnerships rather than rivalries.

Alfred North Whitehead asserts that the aim of the universe, reflecting God's vision, is toward the production of beauty.[4] The quest for beauty leads us beyond cramped and authoritarian visions of God and government, propelling beyond nation-first to world loyalty. God is the artist of the universe, wisely and lovingly creating cells and galaxies As Whitehead notes, "The new, and almost profane, concept of the goodness of God replaces the older emphasis on the will of God...You study [God's] goodness in order to be like [God].[5]

A God whose love is all-embracing inspires persons and nations to become expansive and welcoming, motivated by inclusion rather than banishment, diversity instead of uniformity, adventure above familiarity. God nurtures, as Jesus affirms, those whom we consider friends as well as those we deem enemies, those who are categorized as insiders and citizens, and those whom we consider outsiders and aliens. Transcending small visions of God, motivated by fear and punishment, hate and persecution, we discover that "religion is world loyalty."[6]

Jesus connects perfection with inclusion and wholeness. The ninety-nine sheep, safely in the fold, cannot be whole apart from the hundredth, meandering fearfully in the darkness. The com-

4 Alfred North Whitehead, *The Adventures of Ideas* (New York: Free Press, 1961), 265.
5 Alfred North Whitehead, *Religion in the Making* (Cambridge: Cambridge University Press, 2011), 40.
6 Ibid., 59.

munity can't be complete without finding a place around the table for tax collectors of dubious patriotism, women judged as moral inferiors because of their professions, persons whose health conditions render them the objects of fear and avoidance, and travelers scorned because of their ethnicity.

Jesus knew what it was like to be an outsider on the run. His family were political refugees, running for their lives to escape Herod's death sentence. Apart from the kindness of strangers in Egypt, the Holy Family would have perished. I suspect that Jesus mourned the children slain by Herod in his quest to kill the young Messiah. Today, we can imagine, Jesus' anger and tears at children separated from their parents on USA borderlands, Syrian and Kurdish refugees, pawns in a game between superpowers, fleeing bombs and chemical weapons, LGBTQ youth harassed by classmates and threatened by exclusionary court and legislative decisions, and African American males victimized by the justice system. Surely Jesus was present in the cries of George Floyd to his mother and then his final words, "I can't breathe." God is even with the misguided seventeen-year-old boy who killed two peaceful protesters in Kenosha, Wisconsin. Surely Christ is present in the least of these and Christ challenges the hardhearted and wayward to repent and choose life, abandoning apathy and hate, to become members of God's realm of Shalom. (Matthew 25:31-36)

Jesus' politics, and the politics of those who follow his pathway, goes beyond partisanship and denunciation to inspire inclusion. Jesus was more concerned with hospitality than social mores. Jesus was aware of the feud between Jews and Samaritans and the purity codes that excluded persons with leprosy and tax collectors from worship. The divisions of good and evil were all penultimate, and subject to being discarded when they conflicted with the vision of God who so loved the world that he sent Jesus to reconcile and heal.

The God of Jesus takes us beyond the binary. God loves the sinner as much as the saint. God embraces the wayward as fully as the buttoned-up. God inspires the agnostic as much as the orthodox. What matters in citizenship and public policy is not just affirming our own kin and national sovereignty but the growing recognition that in an interdependent world, all are kin and that although borders must be maintained and laws enacted and enforced, national policies must privilege hospitality, safety, and creativity embracing both citizens and asylum seeker. The nations of the world, Matthew's gospel notes, are not judged by firepower, law and order, or adherence to the mores of the old-time religion, but a deeper more inclusive standard, often scandalous to the moral and civil police of every generation:

> When the Son of Man comes in his glory, and all the angels with him, then he will sit on the throne of his glory. All the nations will be gathered before him...Then the king will say to those at his right hand, "Come, you that are blessed by my Father, inherit the kingdom prepared for you from the foundation of the world; for I was hungry and you gave me food, I was thirsty and you gave me something to drink, I was a stranger and you welcomed me, I was naked and you gave me clothing, I was sick and you took care of me, I was in prison and you visited me." Then the righteous will answer him, "Lord, when was it that we saw you hungry and gave you food, or thirsty and gave you something to drink? And when was it that we saw you a stranger and welcomed you, or naked and gave you clothing? And when was it that we saw you sick or in prison and visited you?" And the king will answer them, "Truly I tell you, just as you did it to one of the least of these you did it to me." (Matthew 25:31-32. 34-40)

CHAPTER SIX

BEYOND IDOLATRY

(Matthew 6:1-18)

Like Lincoln's brief Gettysburg Address, the Lord's Prayer is one of the most profound documents in human history. Like Lincoln's address, which describes the heart of the American experiment, Jesus' prayer on the mountaintop is a systematic theology in miniature, presenting God's relational vision for humankind and the planet. In many ways, the Lord's Prayer is Jesus' spiritual GPS. In living with Jesus' words, we find the way, the truth, and the life in the complexities and challenges of our personal journeys, family and vocational responsibilities, and participation in the broader currents of political life.[7]

Jesus' prayer orients our lives toward God. Not just any god, not Caesar, Nero, or Alexander, but God the Parent. The Infinite is the intimate. God cares. God has skin in the game, like a human parent, and wants the world to flourish, individually and corporately. God is relational. What matters on earth brings joy or sorrow to the "heavenly Parent." But God is more than "my" parent or the parent of my nation. Jesus' God is "our" Parent, the One to Whom All Hearts are Open and All Desires Known." God has no borders and boundaries of love. Though each nation has a unique place in divine providence, God embraces every race, ethnicity, and culture, inspiring and challenging. No nation has a corner on God's love. We can say "God bless the United States of America," but that blessing should be followed by Lincoln's theological caution, "Let us not pray that God be on our side but that we be on God's side."

The Parent who is "in heaven, holy be your name." God is God and you aren't. Nations and leaders will come and go, but God's wisdom and love endure forever. The holiness of God's name critiques every national and political aspiration, especially when

---

7 For more on the Lord's Prayer, see Bruce Epperly *One World: The Lord's Prayer from a Process Perspective* (Gonzales, FL: Energion, 2019) and Robert Cornwall, *Ultimate Allegiance: The Subversive Nature of the Lord's Prayer* (Gonzales, FL, 2010).

leaders and nations assert that they are the chosen ones, called forth to do God's will. Like religion, politics is a matter of life and death, and often political and religious leaders define their chosen candidates and political policies as reflecting God's wishes and their opponents as obstructing God's plan.

In ultimate matters, idolatry is the greatest temptation. We believe that we possess the truth and we must achieve it regardless of the cost to our nation or planet. The current identification of capitalism, climate denial, and anti-abortion stances with God's will is the most recent version of idolatrous identification of our politics with God's. Or, as a placard in mid-America idolatrously proclaimed in the days leading up to the 2020 USA Presidential election, "God, Guns, and Trump."

Jesus' prayer that "your kingdom come, your will be done, on earth as it is in heaven" would have been heard as contrasting God's realm with Caesar's kingdom and other Messianic quests in his time. God's kingdom, or "kindom," as some say, trumps every human political agenda. In a pluralistic society, we do not seek to establish a theocracy or privilege our faith tradition. We do judge our nation and our own political viewpoints in terms of Jesus' prophetic mission statement:

> The Spirit of the Lord is upon me,
> because he has anointed me
> to bring good news to the poor.
> He has sent me to proclaim release to the captives
> and recovery of sight to the blind,
> to let the oppressed go free,
> to proclaim the year of the Lord's favor.
> (Luke 4:18-18)

God's coming realm uplifts the poor, prisoners, vulnerable, and oppressed. God's acceptable or Jubilee year turns upside down our economic structures and challenges the economic gap between the wealthy and poor. The Parent of Us All wants all creation to thrive. Any economic or political policy that marginalizes and impoverishes God's children is an affront to God. God is neither a socialist nor a capitalist. By any just means, God wants the poor to be fed, the homeless to have dwelling places, the sick to be cared for, and the wrongly imprisoned to be set free!

Jesus' prayer turns to bread and indebtedness. Bread matters! Food matters! These words are about providing nutritional as well as spiritual sustenance in Jesus' first-century world in which many lived from meal to meal and a famine could wipe out a community, and our own world in which hundreds of millions of persons lack basic nutrition. Turning from the poor may lead to a famine of hearing God's word among the privileged. God speaks through the cries of the poor and to drown out their pleas with our prayers and praise songs renders us oblivious to God's pleas in our lives. (Amos 8:4-14)

Forgiveness is also essential, especially in the hardscrabble world of politics and economics. We need to reconcile with our enemies, wisely letting go of past hurts, to experience God's amazing world in the present moment. As a child of the prophets, Jesus would have seen the "forgiveness of debts" in economic as well as spiritual terms. God mourns the foreclosing of farms and families being thrown into debtors' prisons. Even in today's USA, approximately 500,000 people a year file bankruptcy as a result of medical bills. Economic justice and a preferential option for the poor, not as morally superior, but as persons in great need, reflects the moral arc of a relational God.

Celtic spiritual guide J. Philip Newell describes "Lead us not into temptation and deliver us from evil" in terms of "Do not forsake us in times of conflict but lead us to new beginnings." The New Zealand prayer book paraphrases: "In times of temptation and test, spare us/From the grip of all that is evil, free us." Politics and civic life are fraught with temptation. Our integrity and honesty are put to risk as we smell the perfume of power. Even our best intentions are ambiguous and can lead to unintended consequences. We pray for purity of heart so that in our fallibility and temptation to control we will remember to seek God's vision "on earth as it is in heaven."

In Jesus' prayer, the personal becomes the political. We pray for guidance, humility, compassion, forgiveness, and justice. We pray for the courage to sacrifice our wellbeing and our nation's individualistic self-interest for the wellbeing of wider and wider circles of community and the planet as a totality. God rules the world with love, challenging us to imitate God's path of relational and loving power in the hard decisions of politics, ecology, immigration, and economics.

CHAPTER SEVEN

THE POLITICS OF SIMPLICITY

(Matthew 6:19-34)

Jesus' Sermon challenges us to self-examination. The mountaintop preacher asks us "what is truly important to us and what are our deepest values? Upon whom do we depend for our living and dying? What values endure the ups and downs of life and civic responsibility? What is our vocation in our personal and political lives?"

Jesus' message was addressed to persons living in a very different culture than our own. The nation was occupied and individuals were powerless politically except as they either aligned themselves with the occupying forces or sought to overthrow Roman oppression. Still, Jesus challenged people to claim their agency. We have inner power, the Spirit within, that enables us to live freely despite the machinations of the powers that be. Intimacy with God inspires courage and self-affirmation, patience with the unchangeable, and agency to transform what is in our power to change.

Jesus' words counseling simplicity and sacrifice as the pathway to peace of mind were likely addressed to the worried well and the anxious affluent in Jesus' audience and not to those on the verge of starvation. Today, they are likely addressed to those of us who are privileged in our society. Our lives are comfortable but we are concerned about the future. Members of the Medicare generation like myself ruminate over Tommy Lee Jones' question, "Will you outlive your money?" despite the fact, unlike the majority world, we own homes and have pensions. Still, we are anxious. We live by visions of scarcity in a world of affluence. We wonder if we have enough and are discontented as we compare ourselves with others. Our sense of contingency and the fragility of life has been magnified by the reality of the COVID-19 pandemic and the possibility that this is the first of many to come.

Mother Ann Seton counseled, "Live simply so others can simply live." Thanksgiving and sacrificial living go together. Recognizing our abundance, we let go of anxiety regarding time, talent, and treasure, strip away the cumber and optional, and rejoice with the birds of the air and the lilies of the field. God provides for their needs and God will provide for ours as well. There is enough for our need not for our greed, as Gandhi asserted. Our divine parent will provide for our deepest needs and challenges us to provide for the needs of others.

Jesus' counsel presupposes a beloved community, in which we let go of self-interest and rugged individualism to experience our largesse as a gift to others and our wellbeing joined with the common good of our community and the planet.

Today, we must read these words in terms of our wanton and intentional destruction of the planetary ecosystem. Conservative Christians have been cheerleaders for climate denial and relaxing environmental regulations. The time is short until Christ comes again, they believe, and in the meantime, we might as well "drill, baby, drill." We don't have to worry about the well-being of future generations because we are the last generation before the Second Coming of Jesus!

Jesus takes a different path from the spiritual materialism and dualistic thinking promulgated by conservative Christian leaders. Jesus lives in a God-filled universe. The heavens declare the glory of God, birds chant praises, Right Whales sport in joyful gratitude, and colorful flowers shout out, "Stop, behold, you are on holy ground." Like the author of Psalm 148, Jesus proclaims the reality of a world of praise in which everything that breathes praises God and "all nature sings, and round me rings the music of the spheres."

Jesus' message calls us beyond anthropocentrism. This is God's world, not ours. The non-human world of sparrows and lilies may be less complex than ours, and have fewer dimensions of experience, but this world of whales, dolphins, chimpanzees, fireflies, and mosquitos has a value apart from human purposes or comforts. Although we must kill to survive, we need to give thanks for the gifts of nature, and practice reverence for life. Wherever we step, we are on holy ground: God loves the baby humans but also the baby whales and fragile monarch butterflies.

Jesus doesn't chart an environmental policy. But he privileges the words of the prophets over short-term profits. Jesus enjoins us to live in a world where creation is revered, where humans are fed and clothed, and every political decision takes into consideration the widest possible circle of wellbeing and the lives of future generations of humans and non-humans alike.

Jesus concludes this section with a challenge and a promise, "Strive first for the kingdom of God and God's righteousness, and all these things will be given to you as well." (Matthew 6:33) Trusting God's abundant universe, and living in solidarity with all creation, we will have all we need. No longer anxious, God's peace will be ours. We will become little Christs and Mahatmas who breathe with the Great Breath of Life and God's everlasting peace will be ours. We will discover that "Peace is self-control at its widest, - at the 'width' where the self has been lost and interest has been transferred to co-ordinations wider than personality."[8]

---

8 Alfred North Whitehead, *Adventures in Ideas*, 285.

Chapter Eight

The Future Belongs to the Intercessors

(Matthew 7:1-12)

Recalling his participation in Freedom Marches with Martin Luther King, Rabbi Abraham Joshua Heschel, noted "I felt as if my legs were praying." The Sermon on the Mount is an extensive guide to prayerful living. For Jesus, prayer isn't something we do occasionally or our conversation with a distant God whom we must coax into caring for us. Prayer is life itself. Every encounter can be a blessing. Each moment is a response to God who constantly addresses us through the events of our lives.

Prayer is the ultimate act of connection, joining us with God and all creation. God wants all of us to have abundant life and our prayers embrace the insight and energy needed to fulfill our dreams. When we align ourselves with God's way, new energies and insights flow into our lives, empowering us to bless the world around us. In gratitude for what we have, we go beyond entitlement and privilege to compassionate care and world loyalty.

Jesus' bold affirmations can best be understood in relationship to the totality of the Sermon on the Mount which roots prayer in our relationship with God and our neighbor. The Lord's Prayer challenges individualistic self-interest, invites us to cancel the debts of impoverished persons, and enjoins prophetic actions to achieve God's vision "on earth as it is in heaven." Honest prayer liberates us from judgmentalism and promotes the solidarity of righteous and unrighteous alike. In the spirit of our calling to embody God's upside down, relational, and all-encompassing realm Jesus promises:

> Ask, and it will be given you;
> search and you will find;
> knock and the door will
> be answered you.
> (Matthew 7:7)

Our asking, seeking, and knocking are responses to God's quest for us. "Listen! I am standing at the door, knocking; if you hear my voice and open the door, I will come in to you and eat with you, and you with me." (Revelation 3:20) Our quest for fulfillment reflects our attentiveness to God's moment-by-moment guidance and inspiration. Moreover, our seeking and finding, and asking and receiving, are not for our benefit alone. Answers to prayer occur in the context of the dynamic interdependence of life and its goal to reflect God's vision "on earth as it is in heaven." Asking in alignment with God's vision takes us well beyond the individualistic "name it and claim it" of the prosperity gospel and the "you create your own realities" of the equally individualistic versions of new thought and new age spirituality.

It is appropriate to "take it to the Lord in prayer," bringing our burdens and cares to God. "The One to Whom All Hearts are Open and All Desires Known" cares about our deepest needs. The Heart of the Universe also challenges us to see our needs as related to the wellbeing of others and the needs of the planet. Our prayers may even drive us to "downward mobility," to prune away our materialistic desires so that others can simply live and experience a lifestyle of abundance appropriate to their context and overall planetary wellbeing.

Prayer is the art of relationship with God and our neighbors. Prayer embodies the golden rule as we seek to "do to others as you would have them do to you" (Matthew 7:12) as well as the great commandments to "Love the Lord your God with all your heart and with all your soul and with all your mind... [and] Love your neighbor as yourself." (Matthew 22:37, 39) The politics of prayer involve praying for those whose policies we abhor as well as those whose policies reflect our values, remembering that we are one in the Spirit despite our political differences and apparent enmity. When we pray for a national leader, prayerful faithfulness requires us to ask that they be blessed with wisdom and health appropriate to achieving the greater good. When we pray for their conversion of heart, we must also confess our complicity in our nation's harmful behaviors. We all need to be driven to our knees in confession and repentance as we seek to turn from the ways of death to the path of life. Ultimately our prayers must include healing of ourselves, others, and the planet through our commitments to God's aim at justice and beauty. Prayer joins us with all creation, the righteous and unrighteous, human and non-human, and not the wellbeing of a select spiritual enclave.

Walter Wink captures the political nature of prayer in his assertion that:

> Intercessory prayer is spiritual defiance of what is in the way of what God has promised. Intercession visualizes an alternative future to the one apparently fated by the momentum of current forces. Prayer infuses the air of a time yet to be into the suffocating atmosphere of the present. History belongs to the intercessors who believe the future into being. Even a small number of people, firmly committed to the new inevitability on which they have fixed their imaginations, can decisively affect the shape the future takes.[9]

Though "the hosts of evil 'round us" the fierce urgency of prayer saves us from "weak resignation to the evils we deplore." Our hope is that God's vision will convict leaders who intentionally sacrifice national parks for short-term profit, deny climate change, blow dog whistles of racism, and traumatize children on our borderlands. Our trust is that protest and prayer, aligning the moral and spiritual arc of history will outlast their machinations. Despite leaders who "scorn thy Christ, assail his ways," God is at work and so we pray "from the fears that long have bound us, free our hearts to faith and praise."[10]

Prayerful protest transforms our lives and the world is transformed. We experience the deep peace which is "self-control at its widest, - at the 'width' where the self has been lost and interest has been transferred to co-ordinations wider than personality."[11] Though the fight be long and we confess our own inability to discern the far horizon, we know that God is with us, calling us to prayerfully march forward, claiming our role as agents in bringing to earth the moral and spiritual arcs of history.

---

9 https://prayerstrategists.files.wordpress.com/2016/01/
historybelongstotheintercessorv1-docx.pdf
10 Harry Emerson Fosdick, "God of Grace and God of Glory."
11 Alfred North Whitehead, *Adventures in Ideas*, 285.

CHAPTER NINE

FINDING THE RIGHT FOUNDATION

(Matthew 7:24-29)

When many of us think of a foundation, we think of something unchanging and solid, the bedrock upon which our homes are built. Some unbending rule of life, inflexible moral judgments untouched by time, separating the good and evil and ensuring that we experience God's favor. Today, we wonder if there is any solid ground to stand on. Postmodernism has challenged every absolute and put at risk timeless truth and doctrine. No truth is final, no path is complete, no fact is uninterpreted. The impact of postmodern relativity is so pervasive that it has engulfed the traditional moral and doctrinal police. Conservative and fundamentalist Christian leaders proclaim the inerrancy of scripture and its moral codes while accepting the machinations of bullying and dishonest leaders as the salvation of the nation. These proclaimers of truth bend the facts to suit their religious-political agenda, embracing factual relativity – alternative facts – while hanging on for dear life to American Christian exceptionalism in the political sphere. Adopting practices they once condemned, they now act as if the "means justify the ends" and sell their souls for a Supreme Court judge who will nullify Roe vs. Wade, discard laws protecting the LGBTQ community, commit human rights violations in separating toddlers from their parents, and promote intolerance to bring public prayer back to school classrooms. In so doing, they have built their houses on the shifting sands, the adoration of political Messiahs, and the idolatry of political and ethical ideology.

Can a theology based on dynamic process and intricate interdependence be an antidote to the impact of Christian exceptionalism in political decision-making? Can a theology that affirms pluralism provide a point of reference for moral and political decision-making? Can process theologians provide a vision that joins tradition and novelty, familiarity and innovation, and unity and diversity, to provide a pathway toward national and planetary healing?

Process theology affirms that God is the most moved mover. God is profoundly concrete, historical, and incarnational. God's power is made perfect in the apparent weakness of ideals that inspire the historical process. "God's mercies are new every morning." (Lamentations 3:23, AP) In the wilderness of our time, "I am about to do a new thing," God proclaims. (Isaiah 43:19) A way will be made, God's vision of Shalom will liberate the people and heal the earth.

The purveyors of Christian exceptionalism cling to yesterday's world and yesterday's God. When they shout "Make America Great Again" at their political revival meetings, they mean to turn back the clock to the days of women at home, gays, and lesbians in the closet, back-alley abortions, and fundamentalist Christianity in the classroom and laboratory. Some cynically assert that what some of the Christian exceptionalists really want is "Make America White Again" as they advocate our nation closing its doors to immigrants of color and promote the growth of white nationalist groups, not unlike the Ku Klux Klansmen who attended church on Sunday morning and burned crosses on Sunday night! While I believe that many conservative Christians are compassionate-spirited in their affirmation of prenatal rights and the return to what they believe to be traditional family values, their political program like all political programs is ultimately ambiguous and fallible.

Process theology takes another path in its political dialogue with Jesus. God is not an authoritarian. God is a companion who rejoices and mourns with us. God is not a dictator. God is a healer who seeks reconciliation and affirmation. God is not a hanging judge, persecuting those with whom we disagree, God is a loving parent and friend, willing to search in the darkness until every lost child is brought home to safety. God doesn't want us to mimic the past. God is the poet of the universe and artist of diversity who wants us to exercise as much freedom and creativity as possible to embody God's new heaven and earth.

As we look at our own faith, rituals, and doctrines, we must confess that "we have this treasure in clay jars, so that it is made clear that this extraordinary power belongs to God and does not come from us." (2 Corinthians 4:7) Our "ultimate allegiance," as

Bob Cornwall asserts, belongs to God, relativizing and concretizing doctrine, practice, ethics, and public policy, whether it be liberal or conservative. Still, we can depend on God to be our firm foundation:

> The steadfast love of the LORD never ceases,
> his mercies never come to an end;
> they are new every morning;
> great is your faithfulness.
> (Lamentations 3:22-23)

God's love is ever new and every fresh. God is constantly altering God's providential care in the call and response of life. When we awaken to God's everlasting and unstoppable love, new possibilities emerge for us, opening the door for God to do greater things in our lives and in the world. God's vision of truth, beauty, and goodness is mated with concrete human life and the affairs of leaders and nations. What is certain is that God's moral and spiritual arc is guiding us forward. God's love is everlasting and all-inclusive, but the shape of that loving embrace and inspiring guidance is always changing, just as our parenting and grandparenting changes depending on the age and maturity of our children and grandchildren.

Today, in our profoundly interdependent world in which we are connected via the media in real-time to people across the globe, there are no strict cultural boundaries and national borders. There is no safe haven off the grid, isolated from climate change, pandemic, and nuclear war. We must build our foundation on God's loving embrace of all creation, God's challenge of isolated individualism, and God's lure toward larger and larger circles of compassion and creativity. While we cannot assume to know God's political will or embody it fully in our laws, our calling is to think globally and relationally and love locally and personally as we claim our very fallible vocation as God's companions in healing the earth and its peoples.

CHAPTER TEN

A TWENTY-FIRST CENTURY SERMON

The practice of preaching has many aims, one of the most important of which is the spiritual formation of preacher and congregant alike. Preaching presents provocative possibilities for personal and relational transformation. Preaching is also a bit like breakfast. We don't remember many sermons specifically, but over a lifetime, preaching – like the least memorable meal of the day – provides theological and spiritual nourishment that transforms our character and behavior, our values, and politics.

Jesus' Sermon on the Mount is a provocative possibility for us just as it was for its first-century listeners. Many went away shaking their heads at its demands that we look at the world and our behavior in radically new ways. How can we embody these impossible ethical commitments? How will we make a living if we put God's economics ahead of our own? How can peace come from humility and sacrifice? Does he really want us, fallible, fearful, and fickle, to be God's companions in healing the world?

We shake our heads, too. We know that Jesus is asking a lot of us – to be his apostles of a new vision of reality. But, without us, the kingdom of God will falter. The stakes are high, God has set before us the ways of life and death, our future and that of our descendants depend on us. We are God's partners and co-creators in healing the earth. We can also be earth destroyers and God must live with our waywardness as well.

> God's purpose is always embodied in particular ide-
> als relevant to the actual state of the world… Every act
> leaves the world with a deeper or fainter impress God.
> He then passes to his next relation to the world with
> enlarged, or diminished, presentation of ideal values.[12]

That is the question, will we give God and our companions a beautiful or ugly world? Will we choose life or death? As we face unprecedented political and social deci-

---

12 Alfred North Whitehead, *Religion in the Making* (New York: Meridian Books, 1972), 152.

sions, Jesus' wisdom is political, personal, and trans-partisan in nature. It is addressed, first, to those who claim to be his followers and then to non-sectarian or agnostic persons of good will who search for a path that gives life to themselves and the planet. Jesus' Sermon presents us with a vision, promise, and practices of personal and planetary healing.

- Jesus' vision describes an interdependent, dynamic, value-laden, enchanted, and lively God-filled world. God addresses us in every encounter, calling us to abundant life for ourselves and others. God's realm needs us to pray, protest, protect, and prevent. We are God's companions in healing the world.
- Jesus promises us that we can experience true peace when we seek first God's realm. Turning to God takes us from anxiety to affirmation, and awakens us to abundant, joyful, and sacrificial living. Attuned to God's vision, we have all the time, talent, and treasure we need to flourish, serve our neighbor, and glorify God.
- Jesus' practices take us from talk to action. Jesus would have affirmed with the Sufi mystic Rumi that there are a hundred ways to kneel and kiss the ground. The Sermon challenges us to lives of self-examination noting where our privilege may be complicit in others' suffering. Jesus tells us to do our inner work so that our actions will bring reconciliation to the world. Prayerfulness is the key to choosing life. Recognizing that God is ultimate, we treasure God's world, honoring our human siblings, living generously and sacrificially, praying our protests, and going beyond binary labels of good and evil, righteous and righteous. Yes, we are to be "perfect" as God is, and our "perfection" is found in compassionate embrace of the earth and its creatures in all their diversity. Perfection does not mean without error, but openness to reflect God's all-encompassing vision as fully as possible in our personal and political lives.

On the mountaintop Jesus presented us with a wide and wise perspective on life, joining us with his Self and all creation. Politics can be cynical, cheap, and power-hungry. Jesus' sermon inspires another kind of politics. Life-affirming politics, bringing heaven to earth, seeking first God's realm, and discovering that we and our nation have everything we need to flourish, grow, and heal the planet and that we can be personally and politically God's companions in healing the world.

CONVERSATION STARTERS

SESSION ONE: CHAPTERS 1-2

1) Recognizing that all politics is local, how do you describe our current political situation? How is it different from Jesus' political context? How is it similar?
2) How does your understanding of Jesus as politically powerless change your understanding of his message? In what ways might the fact that you have political power as a citizen change your understanding of his message?
3) How do you understand Mary's Magnificat? (Luke 1:50-55) In what ways does it challenge our current economic and political system?
4) How do you respond to the Beatitudes found in Matthew 5:1-11 and Luke 6:20-26? In what way are these "blessings?" How might embracing Jesus' blessings change your life?
5) Why is rugged individualism spiritually and politically dangerous?
6) What is your response to Whitehead's description of God as "the fellow sufferer who understands?"
7) What does it mean to be a prophet? In what ways are prophets countercultural? In what ways was Jesus a prophet?

SESSION TWO: CHAPTERS 3-4

1) What is the meaning of light in your spiritual and ethical life? What does it mean for Jesus to call you "the light of the world?"
2) What is the purpose of salt, politically and spiritually? What does it mean for Jesus to call you "the salt of the earth?"
3) What is the right balance of solitariness and social action in spiritual growth?
4) Why is the inner life so important as a catalyst for outward personal and political behavior? How do you respond to Jesus'

words about anger, lust, and forgiveness? Are they impossible to follow?

5) What is your attitude toward non-violent civil disobedience? Is there ever any justification for violating the law?

6) What do you think of Angela Davis' counsel, "I'm no longer accepting the things I cannot change. I am challenging the things I cannot accept"?

7) In what ways do practices like "turning the other cheek" and "going the second mile" transform our spiritual lives?

SESSION THREE: CHAPTER 5

1) What is the meaning of "divine perfection" in the Sermon on the Mount? In your own life, what might perfection mean?

2) How should the USA Constitution's quest for the "more perfect union" shape our nation's public policy?

3) Does the notion of "loving our enemies" have any relevance in the political realm?

4) Does the "golden rule" (Matthew 7:12 have any relevance in public policy? In what ways do national and personal ethics differ?

5) How do our images of God shape our ethics and political policy?

6) What does it mean to say the aim of the universe is toward the production of beauty? How would that statement shape our ethics and public policy?

7) What do you think of Matthew 25's judgment on nations for their treatment of the vulnerable?

SESSION FOUR: CHAPTER 6

1) In what ways does the Lord's Prayer challenge idolatry?

2) What is the most challenging phrase in the Lord's Prayer? What phrase most resonates with your spirituality?

3) In what ways does the Lord's Prayer critique nation-first policies? Economic injustice?
4) What would it mean to have a political process that sought to embody God's will "on earth as it is in heaven?"
5) Although God is not a socialist or capitalist, what do you think of the notion that God has a preferential option for the poor?

Session Five: Chapters 7-8

1) What does it mean to "live simply so others can simply live?" Where do you need to simplify your life?
2) What do you think of the notion that God loves the non-human world and that the non-human world has value and deserves ethical consideration apart from human interests? How do we decide when to favor non-human over human interests?
3) What does it mean to seek first God's realm or kingdom? In what ways does this ensure that we will have everything we need? What is it that we really need?
4) How do you understand the nature of prayer? What does it mean to say, "prayer changes things?"
5) If we understand prayer as social, rather than individual, how do you understand Jesus' invitation to "ask, seek, and knock?" How should we pray for social and political issues? For what outcomes should we pray for?
6) Is it appropriate to join prayer and protest? How shall we pray for political leaders whose policies we deem unjust or dangerous?

Session Six: Chapters 9-10

1) Is there any certainty in a world of pluralism and change? What certainties, if any, do we need to affirm to act courageously?

2) What should our ultimate concern be personally and politically? How should we embody this concern in our citizenship and political advocacy?

3) What do you think of Abraham Lincoln's comment that it is more important that we be on God's side than that God be on ours? How would this shape national policies?

4) What is essential for civil political and ethical conversations in a pluralistic democracy?

5) Do you think our actions shape what God can do in the world? Can we slow down God's aim at justice by our actions? How might we best align ourselves with God's will on earth as it is in heaven?

6) Is it possible to be moral and yet find common ground and compromise in the political world?

7) How do we justify the violence necessary to protect our nation with Jesus' quest for peace in human relationships?

8) Looking back over the past six weeks, how has focusing on the Sermon on the Mount influenced your personal life and politics? What areas do you want to focus on in the future?

Topical Line Drives

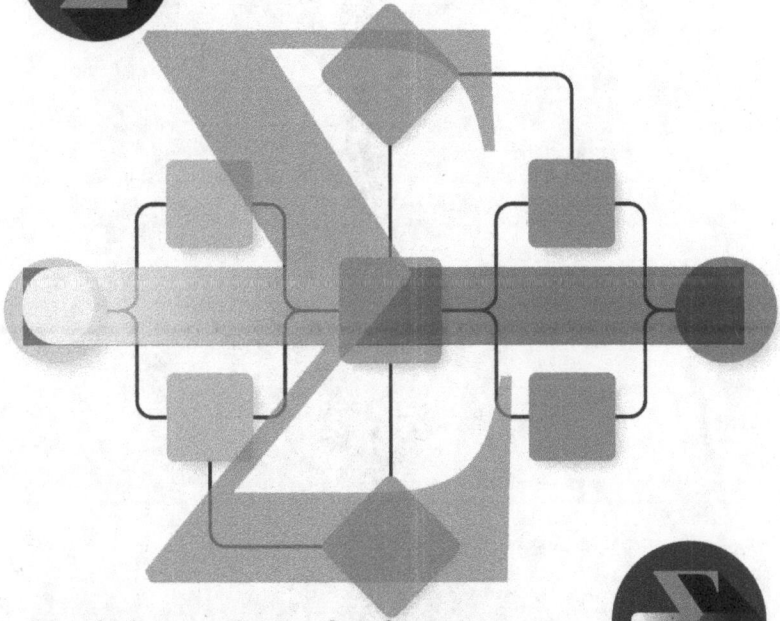

Straight to the point in 44 pages
https://topicallinedrives.com